FRANCIS FRITH'S
TOWN & CITY
MEMORIES

BURY ST EDMUNDS

CLIVE PAINE was born and educated in Bury St Edmunds and
apart from years at university, has worked there all his life. He is
a teacher, lecturer, author and broadcaster on all aspects of local
history. He has taught history and local history for nearly 30 years,
21 of which have been as County Advisory Teacher for Archives
and Local History in Suffolk. He frequently broadcasts on local and
national radio and appeared with Prince Edward on his 'Crown and
Country' series for ITV and has been profiled in 'Readers Digest'.
He is a Council member of the Suffolk Institute of Archaeology
and History; the executive of the Suffolk Local History Council
and part Chairman of the Education Committee of the British
Association for Local History.

NORMAN TOWER 1898 41234

FRANCIS FRITH'S

TOWN & CITY

MEMORIES

BURY ST EDMUNDS

CLIVE PAINE

FRANCIS FRITH'S
TOWN & CITY
MEMORIES

First published as Bury St Edmunds, A Photograph History of your Town in 2001 by
Black Horse Books

Revised paperback edition published in 2005 by Frith Book Company as Bury St
Edmunds, Town and City Memories
ISBN 1-84589-081-7

British Library Cataloguing in Publication Data

Bury St Edmunds
Town and City Memories
Clive Paine
1-84589-081-7

Frith Book Company Ltd
Frith's Barn, Teffont,
Salisbury, Wiltshire SP3 5QP
Tel: +44 (0) 1722 716 376
Email: info@francisfrith.co.uk
www.francisfrith.co.uk

Aerial photographs reproduced under licence from Simmons Aerofilms Limited
Historical Ordnance Survey maps reproduced under licence from Homecheck.co.uk

Printed and bound in England

Front Cover: **BURY ST EDMUNDS, CORNHILL 1898** 41246t
The colour-tinting in this image is for illustrative purposes only,
and is not intended to be historically accurate

FRANCIS FRITH'S

TOWN &CITY

MEMORIES

CONTENTS

THE MAKING OF AN ARCHIVE

Francis Frith, Victorian founder of the world-famous photographic archive, was a devout Quaker and a highly successful Victorian businessman. By 1860 he was already a multi-millionaire, having established and sold a wholesale grocery business in Liverpool. He had also made a series of pioneering photographic journeys to the Nile region. The images he returned with were the talk of London. An eminent modern historian has likened their impact on the population of the time to that on our own generation of the first photographs taken on the surface of the moon.

Frith had a passion for landscape, and was as equally inspired by the countryside of Britain as he was by the desert regions of the Nile. He resolved to set out on a new career and to use his skills with a camera. He established a business in Reigate as a specialist publisher of topographical photographs.

Frith lived in an era of immense and sometimes violent change. For the poor in the early part of Victoria's reign work was a drudge and the hours long, and ordinary people had precious little free time. Most had not travelled far beyond the boundaries of their own town or village. Mass tourism was in its infancy during the 1860s, but during the next decade the railway network and the establishment of Bank Holidays and half-Saturdays gradually made it possible for the working man and his family to enjoy holidays and to see a little more of the world. With characteristic business acumen, Francis Frith foresaw that these new tourists would enjoy having souvenirs to commemorate their days out. He began selling photo-souvenirs of seaside resorts and beauty spots, which the Victorian public pasted into treasured family albums.

Frith's aim was to photograph every town and village in Britain. For the next thirty years he travelled the country by train and by pony and trap, producing fine photographs of seaside resorts and beauty spots that were keenly bought by millions of Victorians.

THE RISE OF FRITH & CO

Each photograph was taken with tourism in mind, the small team of Frith photographers concentrating on busy shopping streets, beaches, seafronts, picturesque lanes and villages. They also photographed buildings: the Victorian and Edwardian eras were times of huge building activity, and town halls, libraries, post offices, schools and technical colleges were springing up all over the country. They were invariably celebrated by a proud Victorian public, and photo souvenirs – visual records – published by F Frith & Co were sold in their hundreds of thousands. In addition, many new commercial buildings such as hotels, inns and pubs were photographed, often because their owners specifically commissioned Frith postcards or prints of them for re-sale or for publicity purposes.

In order to gain some understanding of the scale of Frith's business one only has to look at the catalogue issued by Frith & Co in 1886: it runs to some 670 pages. By 1890 Frith had created the greatest specialist photographic publishing company in the world, with over 2,000 stockists! The picture on the right shows the Frith & Co display board on the wall of the stockist at Ingleton in the Yorkshire Dales (left of window). Beautifully constructed with a mahogany frame and gilt inserts, it displayed a dozen scenes.

POSTCARD BONANZA

The ever-popular holiday postcard we know today took many years to appear, and F Frith & Co was in the vanguard of its development. Postcards became a hugely popular means of communication and sold in their millions. Frith's company took full advantage of this boom and soon became the major publisher of photographic view postcards.

Francis Frith died in 1898 at his villa in Cannes, his great project still growing. His sons Eustace and Cyril continued their father's monumental task, expanding the number of views offered to the public and recording more and more places in Britain, as the coasts and countryside were opened up to mass travel. The archive Frith created continued in business for another seventy years. By 1970 it contained over a third of a million pictures of 7,000 cities, towns and villages. The massive photographic record Frith has left to us stands as a living monument to a special and very remarkable man.

This book shows your town as it was photographed by this world-famous archive at various periods in its development over the past 150 years. Every photograph was taken for a specific commercial purpose, which explains why the selection may not show every aspect of the town landscape. However, the photographs, compiled from one of the world's most celebrated archives, provide an important and absorbing record of your town.

BURY ST EDMUNDS FROM THE AIR 1920
AF1751

BURY ST EDMUNDS BEFORE 1900

The Anglo-Saxon settlement was called Bedericesworth, and lay beside the river somewhere in the present Abbey Gardens. It was here in c630 that Sigeberht, King of East Anglia, built a church after his conversion to Christianity. Bedericesworth now became a royal vill.

King Edmund was executed by the Danes in 869 for refusing to give up his Christian faith. He was shot to death with arrows, beheaded and buried at nearby Bradfield St Clare, and by c892 was regarded as a saint. His body was moved to Sigeberht's royal vill in c900, which became a place of pilgrimage. Over the next 150 years St Edmunds was granted overlordship of the vill and West Suffolk, all of which were to be exempt from most forms of taxation. The rights to hold markets and fairs and to mint coins were also granted. In about 1030 King Cnut replaced secular priests with Benedictine monks, and in c1032 had a round stone church built to house the saint. The boundaries of the settlement were described in a charter of 945; these remained the limits of the Borough until 1934. From about 1000 the settlement became known as St Edmunds, St Edmunds burgh or Bury St Edmunds.

Abbot Baldwin (1065-89) was responsible for laying out most of the grid plan of the town. The Domesday Book in 1086 shows that the town had doubled in value, that 342 houses had been built on former farm land, and that a service industry had developed to serve the monks.

The building of the Abbey church began in 1081 and took over 130 years to complete. The construction of the Abbey resulted in the earlier parish churches of St Denis and St Mary being demolished. They were rebuilt by Abbot Anselm (1122-48) on their present sites as St James's Church in about 1130 and St Mary's Church in about 1140.

The Norman Tower, the original Abbey Gate and the precinct walls were also built by Anselm. By re-siting the churches west of the Abbey, part of Baldwin's town plan had been destroyed, and other alterations probably took place at the same time.

Bury now became one of the major pilgrimage centres in Europe, and the Abbey and the town grew in wealth and status. The Abbot controlled the town and viewed it as the Abbey's 'gift shop'. The markets and fairs made Bury a leading commercial centre in medieval England.

The tight hold of the Abbot over the town led to disputes and conflict. In 1327, for example, the Abbey was sacked by over 3,000 rioters, and the Norman Abbey Gate was destroyed. When (by 1347) the gate was rebuilt, it incorporated a guard room, a portcullis and arrow slits towards Angel Hill (see 41229, pages 18-19).

The Abbey was closed by Henry VIII on 4 November 1539. The whereabouts of St Edmund's body is unknown, but it is most probable that the monks buried it somewhere within the Abbey complex. All the Abbey lands were sold, and Bury took on a new role. Instead of serving the Abbey, it now served the surrounding gentry who purchased the Abbey estates, and became the social and economic centre of West Suffolk. Bury eventually achieved borough status in 1606.

Visitors in the late 17th and 18th centuries commented on the number of substantial houses for the gentry in Bury, the neighbouring estates and the facilities for recreation and trade provided in the town. John Ogilby in 1675 first compared Bury to the health-giving resort of Montpelier, and was later echoed by Daniel Defoe in 1724. Thomas Baskerville in 1681 recorded that Bury was 'a very beautiful inland town, full of rich shops and tradesmen, the streets spacious and the houses well built … gentry do much frequent this town'. Celia Fiennes declared on first sight of Bury that 'the prospect was wonderful pleasant'. Social life centred on the theatre, the Assembly House, and the annual fair, and there was a good coach service to regional capitals and to London.

Economic life in the 18th century was concentrated on the yarn trade. Goods were brought to the town by the Lark navigation from King's Lynn, the place Bury regarded as its port until the late 19th century. Apart from malting and brewing, there was no industry in the 19th century until after the opening of the railway in 1846. The population increased by 45% from 7,655 in 1801 to 13,900 in 1851. By the 1820s, the gradual development of new houses and streets began to the west of the medieval town.

THE CATHEDRAL
CHURCH OF ST JAMES
1929 81951

THE ABBEY RUINS 1929 81944

This is all that remains of the magnificent west front of the Abbey, now reduced in height and stripped of its facing stone. The outline of the three main entrance arches marks the centre of the building. The front would have been twice as high with turrets on the end towers, and with a massive central tower and spire, probably three times the height of the Norman Tower. Beyond the ruins are open countryside and woodland. Since 1979 the town has expanded over the area of Moreton Hall, stretching towards Great Barton and Rougham.

13

Victoria Street, Albert Street and Princes Street, public utilities, industries and churches were built in this area of expansion. These developments included the West Suffolk General Hospital in 1826 (see 41247 p27), Thingoe Workhouse in 1836, the cemetery in 1854 and St Peter's in 1856, all in Hospital Road; the gasworks in 1834 and the sewage station in 1887 at the Tayfen; nearby St John's in 1841 and the railway station in 1847; Cornish and Lloyds engineering works and Gibraltar Barracks of 1878 in Risbygate Street; Robert Boby's engineering works of 1855 and the extension of the cattle market in St Andrews Street; and the electricity generating station on the Playfield in 1900.

THE NORMAN TOWER 1898 41234

This tower was built between 1120 and 1148 as the main entrance to the Abbey, the churchyard and the two parish churches. It was also the belfry for St James's. It was flanked by the high Abbey precinct wall, and the arched entrance with supporting towers formed a porch.

14

BUTTER MARKET C1965 B258095

On market days, Wednesday and Saturday, there are about 100 stalls trading in the Butter Market and Cornhill. Bury is one of the most thriving traditional markets in England. In the 18th century there were at least 18 inns around the market place. One of the last to survive was the Suffolk (right), formerly the Greyhound, which was rebuilt and renamed in 1833. The ground floor was again rebuilt in 1873, including the round arched windows, which were retained after its closure in 1996 when it was converted into two shops.

Angel Hill c1955 B258008

This is the site of Bury Fair, the great social and trading focus of Bury in the late 17th to early 19th centuries. To the left are Abbey House, the 18th-century town house of the Davers family of Rushbrook, the Cathedral and St Mary's. The Athenaeum, or former Assembly House (centre), is little changed since 1802-4, except for the Victorian observatory on the roof. The two buildings to the right were built in 1814-16. One became St Edmund's Hotel, which was acquired by the Angel in 1963.

BURY ST EDMUNDS BEFORE 1900

Improvements in the town centre included a new Corn Exchange in 1836 and its replacement of 1862 (41245 p22-23), new purpose-built banks in Abbeygate Street, and shops of 1886 and a Post Office of 1895 on Cornhill.

Bury was at the centre of five railway lines. It was linked to Ipswich in 1846, to Norwich in 1849 and to Cambridge in 1854. The line to Sudbury functioned from 1865 to 1965, with a second station at Eastgate Street until 1909, and the line to Thetford ran from 1876 to 1960.

ABOVE: THE COUNTY HOSPITAL 1898 41247

The Hospital was established in 1826 in a former ordnance depot built during the Napoleonic Wars, and was virtually rebuilt in 1861. Until 1948 the hospital was voluntary, and wards were named after local benefactors such as Bristol (of Ickworth), Praed (of Ousden) and Hasted (of Bury). In 1847 Dr John Kilner made one of the earliest uses of anaesthesia in an operation. This building was demolished for housing in 1979, and some of the other buildings became Cornwallis Court in 1981. A new hospital was opened in Hardwick Lane in 1974.

THE ABBEY GATE 1898
41229

The original gate was
probably a duplicate of
the Norman Tower. It was
destroyed during the riot
of 1327 and rebuilt in the
Decorated style. The earlier
gate stood to the left of its
replacement, and the join in
the wall shows its position.
The arches on the front had
statues in them, which were
destroyed after 1539.

CORNHILL C1950 B258003

This photograph shows three buildings which typify the prosperity and confidence of Bury in the late 19th and early 20th centuries. From the right they were Thomas the ironmongers, built in 1886, the Post Office of 1895 with the Royal Arms on the gable, and Boots' Tudor fantasy of 1910.

BURY ST EDMUNDS BEFORE 1900

CORNHILL 1898 41246

The Corn Exchange 1898 41245

This was built in 1861-62. The drinking fountain was a gift from the Marquis of Bristol in 1870; it was moved to the Abbey Gardens in 1939 (see B258040, page 70).

COUNTY MAP

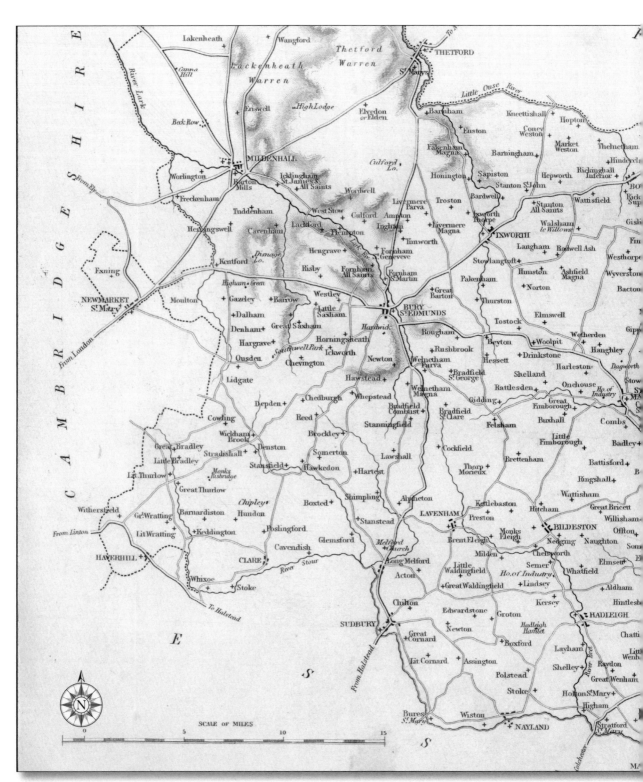

COUNTY MAP

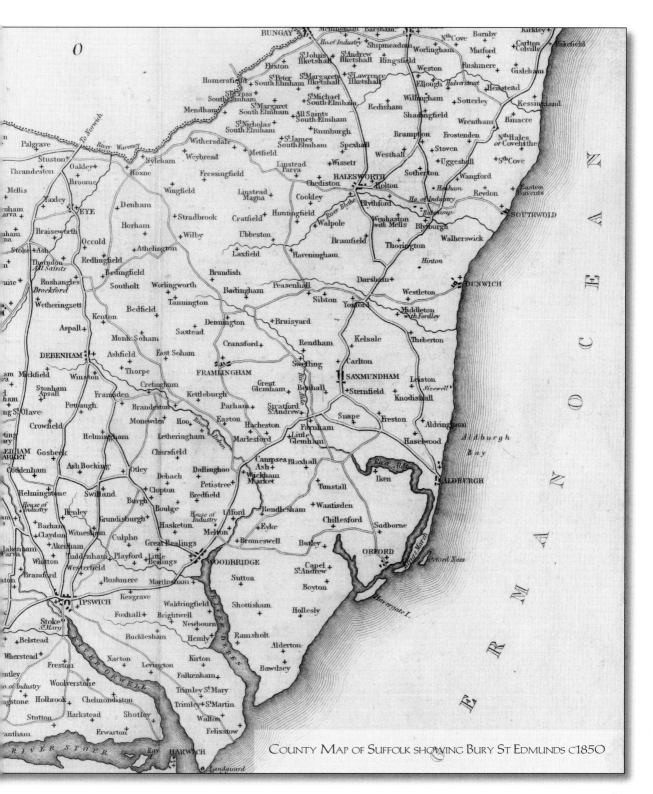

COUNTY MAP OF SUFFOLK SHOWING BURY ST EDMUNDS c1850

Cornhill & Butter Market

Bury was a market and administrative centre before 1066. The large rectangular area now bounded by Abbeygate Street, Butter Market and by Cornhill on two sides was intended to be an open space with market stalls. The west side of Butter Market, Skinner Street and The Traverse mark the lines of former stalls which have become permanent shops and dwellings.

A fire in 1608 destroyed most of the buildings in and surrounding the market place. Many of the later Georgian and Victorian façades mask timber-framed buildings erected after the fire. A Latin verse on Burger King commemorates the fire. It was placed there in the late Victorian period, but probably records an earlier inscription:

> 'Though furious fire the old town did consume,
> Stand this, till all the world shall flaming fume'.

Today the shops are all branches of national chains, and as was the case in most towns, this was a trend that accelerated in the late 20th century. However, some chain stores, such as Lipton's and Stead and Simpson, had been established on the Cornhill by 1896. They were joined by Boots, Maypole, Home and Colonial and International before World War I. Between the wars Woolworth's and Hepworth's moved into Cornhill, and Currys, Dewhurst, Marks and Spencer and Freeman, Hardy and Willis moved into the Butter Market.

Around the market place are some of the finest secular buildings in the town. Moyse's Hall, a Norman stone structure of c1180, is one of the oldest domestic buildings in the country (see B258084 p28-29). It was a merchant's house with a vaulted ground floor for storage and living accommodation above. Original buttresses and a pair of round-headed windows survive. A break in the string course shows where a single Norman window has been replaced. The sill of this later window has a carving of St Edmund's head guarded by the wolf, an image which became part of the borough crest. The building has had a variety of uses, including a workhouse and prison in the 18th century, a police station in 1836, and a railway parcel office in 1892; since 1899 it has been the Museum. Its present appearance with clock and timber belfry dates from 1876.

In the Traverse is Cupola House, built in 1693, as the weathervane declares, by Thomas Macro, an apothecary. Celia Fiennes in 1698 thought this the most up-to-date house in Bury.

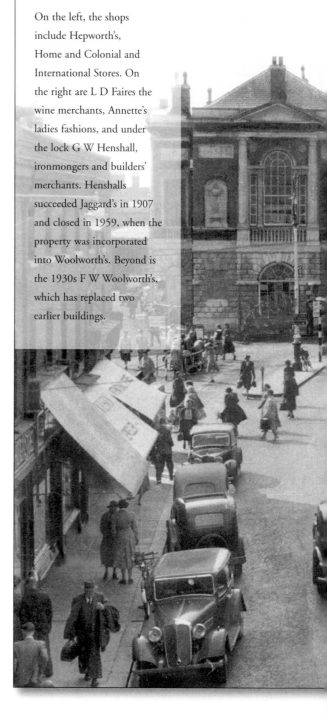

CORNHILL C1955
B258044

On the left, the shops include Hepworth's, Home and Colonial and International Stores. On the right are L D Faires the wine merchants, Annette's ladies fashions, and under the lock G W Henshall, ironmongers and builders' merchants. Henshalls succeeded Jaggard's in 1907 and closed in 1959, when the property was incorporated into Woolworth's. Beyond is the 1930s F W Woolworth's, which has replaced two earlier buildings.

Cornhill & Butter Market

CORNHILL & BUTTER MARKET

On the Cornhill is the magnificent Market Cross (see B258044 p26-27), built in 1774-80 to designs by Robert and James Adam. It encased an existing building, and served as a corn exchange with a theatre above. Unusually for a theatre it occupies an island site, with four identical fronts. There are also panels with masks and musical instruments, representing tragedy and comedy, on two sides. The theatre closed in 1819 and became a concert room - Liszt performed here in 1842. The ground floor was used as a Town Hall between 1849 and 1937. In 1971 the old Town Hall reverted to its original name of Market Cross, and the first floor became the Art Gallery in 1972.

Between Cupola House and the Market Cross is the Corn Exchange of 1836 (see B258001 p32-33), now partly occupied by Laura Ashley. This became an indoor provision market in 1862, and was converted into a school of art and a fire station in 1899. In 1923 the Cullum Reference Library, the bequest of George Gery Milner Cullum of Hardwick House, was established there. The Borough Lending Library was based here between 1937 and 1983 and the fire brigade was here until 1954; it was then based at Fornham Road until 1987, when the new station was opened at Parkway.

The mock-Tudor shop with timber framing, pargetting and statues next to the Post Office (see B258003, p20-21) was originally Boots Cash Chemists. It was designed in 1910 by Michael Treleaven, who created several similar shops for Boots. The statues have a local connection: they are of Agricola, who was present at the defeat of Boudicca, Queen of the Iceni in AD61; St Edmund; Edward I, who held a parliament at the Abbey; and Edward VI, who gave land and money to found the Grammar School in 1550 (it continues as an Upper School). In the central gable a plasterwork panel shows Cnut rebuking his courtiers on the seashore.

As the main trading area of the town, the market place contained a large number of inns. In 1896 there were Everard's Hotel (now Pizza Hut), the Three Kings (Burtons), the Griffin, and the Castle (Superdrug) on Cornhill; the Exchange (Mansfield's), the Victoria (Cupola House) and the Nutshell in the Traverse; the Duke of Edinburgh (McDonald's), the Half Moon (Hughes), and the Suffolk Hotel (Ottakar's and the Edinburgh Woollen Mill) in Butter Market. The Exchange closed in about 1903, the Duke of Edinburgh in 1912, and the Three Kings closed its Cornhill frontage in the 1930s. All the rest closed between 1980 and 1996, leaving Cupola House and the Nutshell as the only remaining pubs in the ancient market place.

BUTTER MARKET c1965 B258084

At the far end, from the left are Lawson's the electricians, who brought television to Bury; Peatling and Cawdron's, wine merchants; the Castle pub; and Moyse's Hall. The spire of St John's can be seen in the distance.

Cornhill & Butter Market

CORNHILL & BUTTER MARKET

CORNHILL C1965 B258086

This photograph, taken 15 years after B258003 (p20-21), shows the new shop mast-head on Boots. The range to the right of the Post Office has been rebuilt as Lipton House. Stead and Simpson have traded from a shop on this site since at least 1898.

CORNHILL & BUTTER MARKET

Cornhill contains the Boer War Memorial. This has a base recording the names of 193 Suffolk men who died 1899-1902, with a bronze statue of a wounded soldier of the Suffolk Regiment. This was unveiled by General Lord Methuen at an impressive ceremony on 11 November 1904. Was the choice of this day a coincidence, or a premonition of war memorials to come?

Bury was raided by German Zeppelins on 30 April 1915 and 31 March 1916, during which seven people were killed in Raingate Street and Springfield Road. On the first occasion mainly incendiary bombs were dropped, and in the Butter Market four buildings were damaged between the Half Moon and the Suffolk. The mock-Tudor building marks part of the site. The detailed local newspaper reports of this raid, and that at Southend on 9 May, led to the Government imposition of a D Notice prohibiting the reporting of air raids.

The Playhouse cinema and theatre in the Butter Market (see B258006 p34-35) was built on the site of the Half Moon, and opened in 1925 with seating for 700. It was here that the first talkies in Bury were heard in 1929 and the first Cinemascope films seen in 1955. This was also the venue for many local drama productions; the best remembered are those of the Bury Amateur Operatic Society. The Playhouse closed in 1959 when the Co-op opened their store, although the Playhouse Bar continued until 1975.

The Playhouse was the third cinema in Bury in the inter-war years. The Empire Picture Palace in the Market Thoroughfare opened in 1911 and burnt down in 1926. The Central opened in Hatter Street in 1924. With three cinemas as rival attractions, the Theatre Royal closed in 1925.

The enormous Odeon opened in Brentgovel Street in 1937 with seating for 1300, with every modern convenience and improved technology. In 1975 it became the Focus, which closed in 1982; it was demolished in 1983, and the site was developed as Cornhill Walk in 1987. The Central became the Abbeygate in 1959 and Studio 1 and 2 in 1971, and continues today as Bury's only cinema.

Cornhill & Butter Market

CORNHILL & BUTTER MARKET

CORNHILL C1955 B258001

On the left is Everard's Hotel with a Greene King dray
outside. The pub had become the Woolpack in 1780 and
Everard's in 1845. It closed in 1987, and was replaced by
Pizza Hut. Woolhall Street, beyond Everard's, marks the
site of the medieval market Toll House and the later Wool
Hall, which was demolished to create the street. The three-
storey building beyond was earlier the Bell Temperance
Hotel. The whole range, including the Eastern Electricity
showroom with the clock, was demolished and rebuilt in
1974-75 with an identical façade. The next building with
the central pediment was Ransomes, Sims and Jefferies,
which became Sainsbury's Supermarket between 1960
and 1987, a shopping precinct and is now Iceland. In
the mid-Victorian period this was Fenton's Old Curiosity
Shop, a second-hand shop taking its name from Dickens's
novel, and looking like Steptoe's living room. The white-
fronted building is the 1933 Burtons, with a billiard hall
upstairs. The building replaced the Three Kings, and its
side entrance still survives. The whole length from Eastern
Electricity up to but excluding Burtons was demolished in
the 1970s, and Central Walk was created to link with the
Cattle Market. A nice survival is the façade of Hunter and
Oliver's, the wine merchants, which was incorporated into
the front of the new Boots in 1977.

CORNHILL & BUTTER MARKET

BUTTER MARKET c1955 B258006

On the left is the covered entrance to the Playhouse. The buildings from the High Spot to the Suffolk were damaged by the Zeppelin raid in 1915, and the timbered Freeman, Hardy and Willis is a 1920s replacement. On the right is Lloyds Bank, built in 1795-97, with Adam-style doors and ground floor windows, as Spink and Carss' Bank. In 1829 it became Oakes and Bevan, in 1899 the Capital and Counties, and in 1918 Lloyds. The bank sign has a beehive for Bevan, and an Oak Tree on top for Oakes of Nowton Park. At the far end is Abbeygate Street, with the three-storey Barclays Bank of 1881, which incorporated the Post and Sorting Office until 1895, the Midland Bank of 1914, and Whipps the fishmonger.

CORNHILL & BUTTER MARKET

ABOVE: BUTTER MARKET C1965 B258085

On the left, Marks and Spencer established a bazaar in 1932, later enlarging and heightening the building several times. The Co-op Bakery and Elite Café (now Saxone) has its awnings out. The building with round-topped windows was W H Smith until 1998, and the next building is the Co-op Quality House, the former Playhouse. On the right Percy Waits succeeded Smart and Farries in 1947. The next four smaller shops are Dewhurst's, Meeson's, Annette's and the Singer Shop. The next large shop front covering two buildings is Pretty's the Drapers, which was here since the 1890s. The shopfront dates from a refitting of 1927. At the end of the street the Midland Bank took over Whipps in 1963 and extended the bank over the site.

ABBEYGATE & CHURCHGATE STREETS

In 1971, John Betjeman wrote: 'The most perfect and least-spoiled English town, reminiscent of the time of Jane Austen, is Bury St Edmunds'.

Abbeygate has undergone a number of changes in name. In 1433 it was divided into trading areas called Fishmarket, Spicer Row, Barber Row and Cook Row. Eventually the whole length became Cook Row, and in 1792 the name was changed to Abbeygate Street.

As everywhere in the heart of Bury, despite the Georgian and Victorian appearance of the buildings, most of them are timber-framed with later façades. Here good examples of timber buildings can be seen at Lloyds the chemists, which has a carved corner post and a wealth of timber in the ceiling, and at the late 15th-century Norwich and Peterborough, which has carved jetties on three sides.

Several of the larger buildings were purpose-built in the Victorian and Edwardian period. These include at the top end, the Italianate-style National Provincial Bank of 1868 (now the Alliance and Leicester) and the Jacobean-style Alliance Assurance of 1891 of red brick with Dutch gables (Café Rouge) - see B258002, right; the Renaissance-style Barclays Bank of 1880 (HSBC); and the Corn Exchange of 1862 (see 71954 p40-41). On the corner of Hatter Street is the Queen Anne-style West Suffolk Country Club of 1883.

The number of retail outlets has remained at about 47 or 49 between 1896 and 2001, whilst the range of services available from these outlets has declined from 24 in 1896 to 20 in 2001. By 1941 half the shops were selling the same type of goods as in 1896, of which 70% were still trading under the same name. A comparison of 1896 with 2001 shows that clothing shops remained at 25% of the total; food and drink increased from 19% to 21%; chemists declined from 8% to 2% and banks and building societies increased dramatically from 6% to 16%.

All the grocers have closed since 1941. Walker's is now the Norwich and Peterborough; the Star is now Going Places; Oliver's is Baker's Oven, the International is now the Abbey National; and Ridley's is Caffe Uno. The most significant difference is that in 1941 all but one of the food shops sold provisions to cook at home; now, all but one are restaurants. Perhaps Abbeygate Street has become Cook Row again.

Seven shops and a bank remain from 1900. These are Palmer's (Plumpton's), Thurlow Champness, Collis's, Thresher's (Hunter and Oliver), Barwell's, Dudley Mason's (Quant's), Lloyds (Skoulding's)

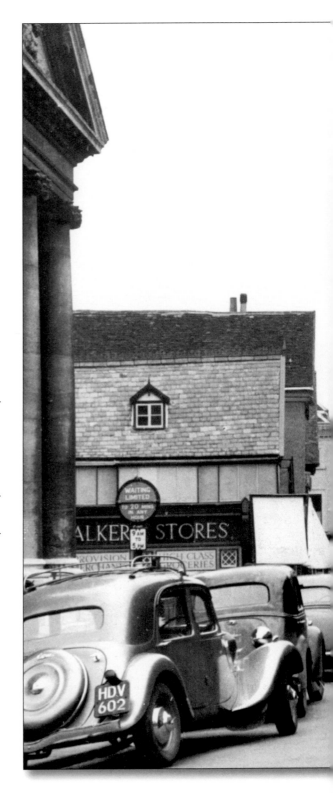

ABBEYGATE & CHURCHGATE STREETS

ABBEYGATE STREET C1955 B258002

On the left is Walkers Stores with the tiled advertisement 'Provision Merchants and High Class Groceries'. The higher gable beyond is Cross the florist, whose nursery was at Chapel Farm on Hollow Road. On the right are the National Provincial bank, the Alliance, and the mock-Tudor front of Henley's children's shop, which lost a gable width in 1891 when the Alliance was built. On this corner is the International, and beyond is Jenkins the chemists, in a building that has been a chemists since 1798.

ABBEYGATE & CHURCHGATE STREETS

ABBEYGATE STREET C1965 B258094

The new ground floor shopfront of Plumpton's is on the left, followed by three shop signs on Oliver's, Burdon's and Thurlow Champness. On the right is the entrance to Gross and Co, solicitors, and to the Register Office, which was in use until 1982. The shop front of Quant's dates from 1930.

ABBEYGATE & CHURCHGATE STREETS

and Barclays Bank.

Georgian shop fronts survive on two of the former grocers, now Baker's Oven and Caffe Uno. Two adjoining shops still have Victorian trade signs. Leeson's has a mortar and pestle on the former chemists' shop founded in 1831 as Nunn, Hinnell, Clark and Burdon. Thurlow Champness has a large decorative clock made by William Potts of Leeds in 1900.

Opposite is Quant's former shoe shop, now Dudley Mason's, established in 1858. One of the Quants was a founder member of the Baptist Church in 1800. The company invented a revolutionary design for children's shoes, 'Startrite', in 1921, and had installed an x-ray machine to view children's feet inside their shoes in 1955. This made the purchase of a new pair of shoes an exciting and technological experience.

The Corn Exchange of 1861-2 dominates the top of the street (see 71954, right). The site was formerly occupied by the Georgian butcher's shambles, one section of which survives at the north end with a Doric colonnade and pediment. The building was constructed ten years after the Great Exhibition, and uses the same curved and glazed roof structure supported by iron girders. The portico, with six Ionic columns, has a central medallion with Queen Victoria's head, flanked by figures and images representing livestock and labour and the prosperity and abundance of that labour, with the inscription 'The Earth is the Lord's and the Fullness Thereof'.

The building was used as an Exchange on Wednesdays, and also as a public hall for concerts, sales and entertainments including dancing, wrestling and roller-skating. In 1969-70 a first floor was inserted and shops were built into the ground floor, of which G Boughton's is the only original occupant.

On 16 June 1882 half the section of the street between Hatter Street and Angel Lane was destroyed by fire. The buildings lost were the West Suffolk County Club tobacconist's, butcher's, photographer's, greengrocer's and draper's shops. The owner of the tobacconist's was eventually sentenced to five years for attempting to defraud his Insurance Company. New buildings were erected set back from the original building line (see B258007, p44), which is why part of the gable end of No 38, now Strides, is exposed and appears to jut out on to the pavement.

ABBEYGATE & CHURCHGATE STREETS

THE CORN EXCHANGE 1922
71954

The urns have been removed from the parapet, and a new doorway inserted since 1898. Everard's Commercial Hotel is to the left, and in the distance is the earlier Corn Exchange of 1836. To the right is the cupola of Cupola House. In the foreground Charles Tozer, house decorator, of Orchard Street, is at work on the present Saffron Laundry. Just out of the picture is the Nutshell, reputed to be the smallest pub in England.

ABBEYGATE & CHURCHGATE STREETS

ABBEYGATE STREET c1955 B258007

The shop on the left is Jarman's the photographers. It was designed by William Spanton in 1863 for his 'Repository of the Arts' and was owned by Harry and Oswald Jarman from 1901 to 1962. There can be very few wedding photographs taken between 1901 and 1975 that do not bear their signature. Next are Groom's stationers and booksellers run by the Groom sisters; Hilton's Shoes and Collis the jeweller occupy the building with Venetian-style oriel windows. The three businesses beyond were the garage of T H Nice, the Gallon Pot pub, and Hunter and Oliver, wine merchants, later to be Peter Dominic and now Thresher's. On the right is the length of the street rebuilt after the 1882 fire. If we stand at the same spot today, we still look out over open countryside.

ABBEYGATE & CHURCHGATE STREETS

BELOW: CHURCHGATE STREET 1929 81937

This photograph shows the more residential character of this street. A rare tin sign for Arthur
Rozier, tin and zinc worker, is on the 16th-century jettied building to the left. The brick
building in the right foreground is an example of early 19th century infill - this plot was a
garden on Warren's map of 1791. Lower down beyond the children is the corner drapery shop
of the Misses Pryke.

ABBEYGATE & CHURCHGATE STREETS

ABOVE: CHURCHGATE STREET C1955 B258076

On the right are the Edwardian buildings occupied by Marlow's from 1925 to 1975, Watson's Post Office and the Queens Head. This had been the Norfolk Coffee House; it was rebuilt in white brick in 1838. On the left all the buildings are timber-framed, although several have later brick frontages: for example the grocer's shop, now Gavin Ashley's, is dated 1835. The awning indicates Land's High Class Furnishings and Removals, which were established here between 1905 and 1981. The wooden gilded Hovis sign is on Berry's the bakers, trading here from 1906 to 1999, and noted for their quality bread made in a Georgian oven.

LEFT: CHURCHGATE STREET C1965 B258087

On the left is the former Presbyterian Chapel, now Unitarian Chapel, of 1711. To the right the ground floor below the jetty of the 16th-century house was partly rebuilt in the early 19th century, when the sash windows were inserted.

Abbeygate & Churchgate Streets

Churchgate Street runs parallel to Abbeygate Street. Its line continues through the Norman Tower to the central entrance of the Abbey. Although we have no actual evidence, it would seem logical to suppose that this was one of the main routes for pilgrims to the shrine of St Edmund. Churchgate Street did not develop into a trading complex as Abbeygate Street did. In 1896, 1941 and 2001 only 35% of the properties have a commercial use. Then as now, most of these were in the central section between Hatter Street and Bridewell Lane. The number of trades and services available had declined slightly from 22 in 1896 to 18 in 1941 and 17 in 2001. Today, apart from the Queens Head, only Bloomfield's shoe shop has the same function and name as in 1896.

It was in Churchgate Street in 1711 that the first Nonconformist chapel in Bury was built by the Presbyterians (see B258087 p44). This is an impressive red brick structure in English bond, using alternate courses of stretchers and headers. The front is as opulent as the façade of a country house. The central doorway is flanked by large round-headed windows, and above is a delicately glazed elliptical window. The chapel was restored in 1991 and is used for meetings, concerts, and Unitarian worship. The interior still has the galleries with box pews and the double-decker pulpit and tester facing the door.

In 1903 a fire destroyed the premises of Hervey's the grocers. In its place H S Watling of Bury designed a large three-storey building in mock Medieval Tudor style (see B258076, p45). Marlow's timber merchants, who started here with six men and a handcart, took the building over in 1925. By 1970 the company had outgrown the site, and in 1975 they moved to Hollow Road.

The Norman Tower 1929 81948

The building on the right was designed by Lewis Cottingham in 1846 as the Penny Bank, which functioned until 1892. This and the adjoining Tower House in the churchyard are wonderful examples of early Victorian Gothic revival architecture. To the left is the former Six Bells, with a lovely brick front masking an 18th-century timber structure. The inn closed in 1885 and was sold in 1890; it was converted into a Masonic lodge.

ANGEL HILL & CROWN STREET

BURY ST EDMUNDS

ABOVE: DETAILS FROM B258071, 81945 AND B258077

'Is this Bury St Edmunds? - It is, replied Mr. Pickwick. The coach rattled through the well-paved streets of a handsome little town, of thriving and cleanly appearance, and stopped before a large inn situated in a wide-open street, nearly facing the old abbey. And this, said Mr. Pickwick, looking up, - is the Angel'. Thus in 1836 Charles Dickens brought Mr Pickwick to the Angel Inn on Angel Hill.

This large rectangular open space, in front of the secular part of the Abbey, was used as a fairstead, and was originally called the Mustowe, or meeting place. The earliest known use of the name Angel Hill for

ANGEL HILL & CROWN STREET

ABOVE: THE ANGEL HOTEL AND THE ATHENAEUM C1965 B258078

To the left, Crown Street runs up towards St Mary's and Greene King's brewery. On the right is the direction sign of 1935, which was known as 'the Pillar of Salt'.

this area is in 1663. In the 18th century, Bury Fair, held on Angel Hill in October, was one of the most fashionable and largest trading fairs in the country. Around the edge of the area were the Assembly House, the Angel and large houses of the gentry and wealthy tradesmen.

The fair attracted traders from London and the provincial capitals. They either had stalls or booths, or they hired ground-floor rooms of buildings in the surrounding streets. There were also exhibitions and entertainments, including Wombwells Menagerie, a learned pig, human dwarfs and giants and even an invisible girl! In the late 18th century, the fair was described as 'the rendezvous of the Beau Monde every afternoon, who conclude the evenings by the Plays or Assemblies. This fair consists chiefly of several rows of Haberdashers, Milliners, Mercers, Jewellers, Silversmith and Toy shops, which make a fine show'.

A poem by George Bloomfield in 1816 described the entertainment centred on the Assembly House and the theatre:

'And those who are rich will surely repair
To Bury to taste the delights of the fair
The Elegant Ball Room formed to display
The sparkling claims of the Rich and the Gay
Theatrical Views, the fine Mimic art
Are in perfection their charms to impart'.

However, a long period of decline in trade at the fair began in the 1830s, which was accelerated by the railway in the 1840s. The fair was eventually abolished in 1871 as a public nuisance.

ANGEL HILL & CROWN STREET

BELOW: ANGEL HILL C1955 B258049

The gateway to the Abbey and the commercial edge of the secular town face each other across Angel Hill.

Angel Hill & Crown Street

Above: The Angel Hotel 1929 81945

The Virginia creeper on the Angel is beginning to cover the new first floor, which was built in 1921-22 over the garage entrance. The 16th-century gabled and timber-framed building beyond has a 20th-century Regency-style shopfront, and was called Pamela's for many years. The tall 18th-century building is Norman's chemist's shop, later to become Leesons; its shopfront with an Ionic colonnade was added in 1834. In the distance we can see scaffolding on a house - it was destroyed by fire in September 1929.

ANGEL HILL & CROWN STREET

The Assembly House had been one of the main social centres of Bury since the early 18th century. The building then had a third storey, and an Adam-style ballroom was added in 1789. Between 1802-04 the building was altered to its present appearance to the designs of Francis Sandys, who was also responsible for the Rotunda at Ickworth, and the building was re-named the Subscription Rooms. Here the gentry and the 'better sort' met to dance, play cards, take tea and assemble together. Events were held to coincide with the sitting of the Courts of Quarter Session and Assize, and the fair, all of which drew in large numbers of the gentry.

In 1830 William Cobbett in his 'Rural Rides' described Bury as 'the nicest town in the world ... it is the neatest place that ever was seen. It is airy, it has several fine open places ... and it is so clean and neat that nothing can equal it'. Thomas Carlyle in 'Past and Present' (1843) commented that Bury was 'a prosperous brisk Town, beautifully diversifying with its clean brick houses and ancient clean streets'.

In 1854 the Athenaeum Literary Institute purchased the Subscription Rooms, and after a lecture in 1859 by the Astronomer Royal, Sir James Airy of Playford, the observatory was added. The ballroom doubled as a lecture hall, and the building also contained a library and natural history museum. In 1935 the Athenaeum was acquired by the Borough Council.

The Angel was rebuilt between 1774 and 1777 as a three-storey building with an Adam-style porch and a pedimented parapet. A carriage entrance was added in 1818, and in 1921-22 the hotel accommodation was extended over it, matching the original design (see 81945 p50-51). Dickens stayed at the Angel in 1859 and in 1861, when he gave public readings of his work at the Athenaeum. He later described Bury as 'a bright little town'.

Two major fires occurred on Angel Hill in the early 20th century. In May 1912, No 9 Angel Hill was burnt down; it is marked by the space next to Angel Corner. On 5 September 1929 a Queen Anne house was destroyed with loss of life, and the Borough Offices were later built on the site (see 81945, p50-51, and B258077, p54). These were opened in April 1937, and the mock-Georgian style of the building, designed by local architects Mitchell and Oliver, was used for most of the early post-war local authority housing on the Mildenhall Estate after 1946.

THE WAR MEMORIAL 1922 71955

This photograph was taken after Armistice Day 1922. The Queen Anne house, built in 1702 and presented to the National Trust in 1943, became known as Angel Corner in 1956. It housed the Bury and West Suffolk Record office from 1953 to 1973, and the John Gersham Parkington Memorial Clock Museum from 1953 to 1992. The house has since become the Mayor's Parlour. To the left is part of the garden wall of the house destroyed by fire in 1929.

ANGEL HILL & CROWN STREET

ABOVE: ANGEL HILL c1965 B258077

The 'Georgian' Borough Offices of 1937 dominate this view
from Mustow Street. The buildings to the left include timber-
framed structures, at least four of which have jettied first floors.
Bell's furnishers dates from c1500, and since 1985 has had
all its timbers exposed. The 1930s Burrell's garage had petrol
pumps on the pavement installed in 1923; these were the first
in Bury. Three different types of advertisements are displayed:
Bell's plays on its name, claiming 'Bells for sound furniture';
the 16th-century One Bull has a sign showing a Papal Bull; and
Burrell's has a square clock. The three-storey building on the
left-hand corner was built in 1849 to replace the Globe, which
had succeeded the earlier Cock and Pye Inn.

ANGEL HILL & CROWN STREET

BELOW: THE ABBEY GATE AND ANGEL HILL C1960 B258072

This photograph shows the range of substantial brick-fronted Georgian houses at the north end. Opposite is the curving early 19th-century Crescent House, which included Mem's Café, 'the place where friends meet', and Honor Bright, home-made chocolates. The buses are a reminder that independent bus companies, including Chamber's, Cutting's, Goldsmith's, Mulley's, Simond's and Theobald's, used this area.

CROWN STREET 1929 81935

This view is taken from the Norman Tower looking south. Beyond Westgate Street lies woodland and countryside, including Hardwick Heath. Today most of this area is covered by housing, part of the expansion of the town since the mid 1970s. On the left is Tuns Passage. The former Three Tuns Inn, which closed in 1903, became the St Mary's Institute until 1949 and was then the Labour Party office until 1997. The complex of buildings at the far end of the street is part of Greene King brewery. The three malt houses were replaced in the 1950s, and the chimney was demolished in the 1980s. The roofline of the Theatre can be seen at the end of the left-hand side of the street.

ANGEL HILL & CROWN STREET

As Angel Hill is the main public square in the town, the war memorial (see 71955 p52-53) was sited here in 1921. The Celtic cross was unveiled by General Lord Horn and dedicated by Bishop David on 13 October 1921, in the presence of several thousand people. The speeches drew attention not only to the sacrifice of those commemorated but also to the Zeppelin raids, the long links between the Suffolk Regiment and its garrison town, and the work of the local Red Cross Hospitals, including the one in nearby Northgate Street.

Another feature on Angel Hill is the illuminated Art Deco direction sign erected in 1935. It gives directions to Ipswich, Stowmarket, Sudbury, Mildenhall, Thetford and Yarmouth. Until the early 1970s when the Bury by-pass opened, most of the through traffic passed this sign.

Running south from Angel Hill is Crown Street, leading to Westgate Street, with the Brewery and Theatre Royal (see 81935, left). The Greene King Brewery is an amalgamation (1887) of Westgate Brewery, founded by Benjamin Greene in 1800, and St Edmund's Brewery, started by Frederick King. It developed into one of the main regional breweries in the county. In 1890 it had 260 public houses; it had 482 in 1929 and 512 in 1954.

The Theatre Royal was designed as the New Theatre in 1819 by William Wilkins, later to be the architect of the National Gallery, and was renamed the Theatre Royal in 1845. It closed in 1925 as a result of competition from the cinemas, and became a barrel store for Greene King. In 1965 it re-opened; it is the third-oldest surviving Regency theatre in the country. The premiere of 'Charley's Aunt' was performed here in 1892 - the play includes the immortal words 'I'm Charley's aunt from Brazil, where the nuts come from'.

ANGEL HILL & CROWN STREET

ABOVE: THE DOG AND PARTRIDGE HOTEL 1929
81947

In the 18th century this was the Mermaid, but it had
become the Dog and Partridge by 1791. Despite being
a 17th-century timber-framed building, it was given a
mock-Tudor make-over, which was shortly to be removed
- see B258071, right.

RIGHT: CROWN STREET c1955 B258071

The Dog and Partridge (centre left) looks much as it does
today. To the left of the pub is the site of the house where
Abbot John Reeve lived from the closure of the abbey in
November 1539 until his death in April 1540. The three
houses to the right of the pub show the variety of styles
and materials in the street. One is early 19th-century,
built in white Woolpit or Culford brick, with a doorway
with Doric columns (the house opposite has a porch with
similar columns); next is a 17th-century timber-framed
building with a jetty and dormer windows; the third is
a building re-fronted to disguise the jetty and to appear
Georgian, with a classical door case.

Brabner's Map

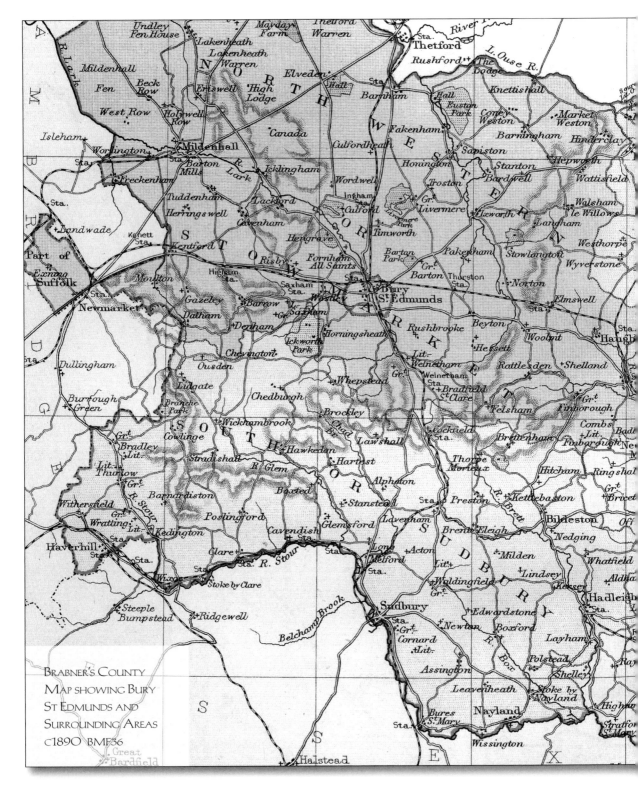

Brabner's County Map showing Bury St Edmunds and Surrounding Areas c1890 BMF36

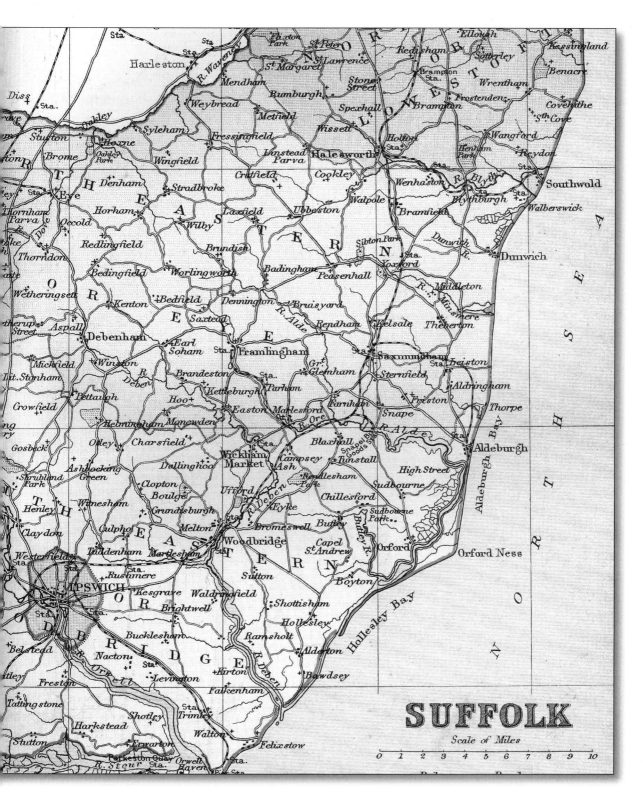

SUFFOLK

Scale of Miles

0 1 2 3 4 5 6 7 8 9 10

THE CHURCHYARD & ABBEY GARDENS

THE ABBEY RUINS 1898 41228

Houses had been built into the central arches of the west front by at least the 1660s. The Norman-style windows to the right date from 1863, when this wing became the Probate Registry Office. In 1957 the Borough Council purchased the ruins from the Bristol family, as part of the scheme to turn the area into a cathedral close. The monuments were removed in 1958, and the area was laid to lawn. A statue of St Edmund, by Dame Elizabeth Frink, was placed here in 1976 to commemorate the end of Bury St Edmunds and West Suffolk as independent administrative areas.

The Churchyard & Abbey Gardens

The churchyard was enclosed by the precinct walls of the Abbey to the south and west between 1120 and 1148, and was used for the burial of the townspeople. After 1539 the churchyard passed into private ownership, although it was still used for burials. The Borough purchased the area in 1798 and it eventually closed in 1854, when the cemetery in Hospital Road was opened. There are about 1,200 surviving gravestones, the earliest of which is dated 1637. The churchyard is carefully managed as a haven for wild life and vegetation in the heart of the town.

The Charnel Chapel was used as a site for later monuments. Among them are those to Mary Haselton, who was killed aged nine in 1785 by a flash of lightning whilst saying her evening prayers; Sarah Lloyd, a servant of Hadleigh, who was hanged in 1800 for house robbery; and Henry Cockerton (who died in 1853), the author of 'Valentine Vox the Ventriloquist'. Sarah Worton's epitaph is a dire warning:

'Good people all as you Pas by,
Looke round and see how corpes do lye
For as you are sometime Ware We
And as we are so must you be'.

From the early 18th century the churchyard became a place of display and promenade for the gentry and 'better sort', and from 1820 to 1831 the Botanic Gardens were at the east end. Two of the avenues of trees were planted before 1832; they led from the side doors of the two churches, and from the Norman Tower to the Shire Hall. The other two avenues, running from the Norman Tower in front of the Dean's House, were planted between 1863 and 1885.

Adjacent to the churchyard, and facing each other across it, are two substantial Georgian houses. On the north is Clopton's Asylum, now the Dean's house, built in 1735; it was the bequest of Dr Poley Clopton, as an almshouse for 12 decayed gentlefolk. In 1897 it became the Vicarage of St James's. On the south is the Manor House, built in 1736-38 to the designs of Sir James Burrough as the town house of Lady Elizabeth Hervey of Ickworth. The house has had a variety of owners and uses, including as a Preparatory School (which the author's wife attended), and as a County Council and Petty Sessions Offices. In 1988 it was purchased by the Borough and opened as a museum in 1993.

IN LOVING MEMORY
OF THE
SEVENTEEN PROTESTANT MARTYRS,
WHO FOR THEIR FAITHFUL TESTIMONY TO GOD'S TRUTH,
DURING THE REIGN OF QUEEN MARY,
SUFFERED DEATH IN THIS TOWN, 1555-1558.

THIS MONUMENT,
PROVIDED BY PUBLIC SUBSCRIPTIONS,
ERECTED, A.D. 1903,
WAS UNVEILED ON DECEMBER 22ND BY
THE DEAN OF CANTERBURY
(THE VERY REV. HENRY WACE, D.D.)

THE NOBLE ARMY OF MARTYRS
PRAISE THEE O GOD.

THE CHURCHYARD & ABBEY GARDENS

NOTICE
THIS ROAD IS NOT
TO BE USED BY
VEHICLES OR CYCLISTS
BY ORDER

THE MARTYRS'
MEMORIAL 1929 81943

The monument of 1903
commemorates 17 Suffolk
Protestants who were burnt
at Bury during the reign
of Queen Mary. The ruins
of the Charnel Chapel are
between the two avenues.

THE SHIRE HALL 1929 81950

The Shire Hall was rebuilt in 1907 in an Edwardian classical style, which included the arms of West Suffolk over the doorway. It was designed by A A Hunt of Bury.

THE CHURCHYARD & ABBEY GARDENS

THE ABBEY GARDENS AND THE ABBEY GATE 1898 41230

The gardens were described in 1891 as 'laid out in a circle… with various radiating beds intersected by principal promenades and many green paths, and are kept constantly filled by masses of the gayest flowers'.

Also within the churchyard is the Shire Hall (see 81950, left), the administrative and judicial centre of West Suffolk since the Dissolution. Here in 1722 Arundel Coke was tried for the attempted murder of his brother-in-law Edward Crisp in the churchyard. He was found guilty of maiming and hanged. Here, too, in 1800 Sarah Lloyd was sentenced to death; and in 1828 William Corder was found guilty of the murder of Maria Martin in the notorious Red Barn.

The Abbey Gardens includes the site of the church, the Abbot's Palace and all the other buildings and grounds associated with the Abbey. The area was in private ownership from 1539 until 1953.

Queen Elizabeth I stayed in the former Abbot's Palace in 1578; the next Royal visit, by Edward VII in 1904, took place outside the Abbey Gate.

Moved from its original site, the Botanical Gardens (41230, above) were established here in 1831 by Nathaniel Hodson, who obtained a lease of the area from the owner, the Marquis of Bristol. They were modelled on the Royal Botanic Gardens in Brussels, with an inner and outer circle of beds, with lawns and gravel walks. The entrance was from the Abbey Gate with the main walk, as today, leading down to the river, with a second walk crossing at right angles. Admission to the gardens was by an annual subscription, or daily

67

THE CHURCHYARD & ABBEY GARDENS

THE ABBEY GARDENS C1965 B258082

Excavations were carried out on the Chapter House in 1902, when the graves of five Abbots, including that of Abbot Sampson, were discovered. A major excavation and repair of the Abbey church was undertaken in the 1960s and 1970s.

THE NORMAN TOWER c1955 B258069

Much of the Abbey would have been designed with arches, openings and decorations similar to those that survive on the Norman Tower. The precinct wall would have originally closed the gap between the Tower and St James's. In the 18th century the Widow's Coffee House stood here, run by Mary and Letitia Rookes. There is no evidence whatsoever that this was also a brothel.

payment. A variety of waterfowl, pheasants, rabbits and guinea pigs was introduced in 1835, the predecessors of the aviaries established against the north precinct wall in the 1950s.

As a result of the 1907 Pageant, funds were available for the Borough to lease the gardens in 1912, and open them as a public park. To celebrate the coronation of George VI in 1937, the gardens were redesigned within the earlier circular plan. The beds forming concentric circles in the centre were replaced with the present island beds, which contain two different displays each year. In 1953 the Borough purchased the whole area of the Abbey Gardens. The high standard of horticulture and design has greatly contributed to Bury winning the Britain and Europe in Bloom several times since 1987.

A rose garden to the east of the cathedral (B258041, p71) is maintained by the royalties arising from 'Suffolk Summer', written in 1948 by John Appleby, an American serviceman based at Lavenham airfield from 1943 to 1945. The garden consists of rose beds surrounded by mellow walls and yew hedges, and contains several USAAF war memorials. The garden links the tranquillity and continuity of an English garden with the horror and sacrifice of the war zone.

King Edward VI Grammar School occupied a site on the Vinefields adjacent to the Abbey Gardens from 1883 until 1971 (see 41244, p72). The school was founded in 1550 in Eastgate Street (now the Ancient House), and moved in 1665 to Northgate Street (St Michael's Close) and to the Vinefields in 1883.

The Grammar School became a Direct Grant school in 1922 and a Voluntary Controlled school under the Local Education Authority in 1946. The school closed in 1971 at the time of comprehensive reorganisation, and became St James's Middle School. There was always a boarding department: the author's wife Dorothy was its last matron at the time of its closure in 1969. The old name still continues as King Edward VI Upper School, which occupies the former Silver Jubilee buildings in Grove Road.

THE SUNDIAL c1955 B258040

The 1870 drinking fountain was moved here from the Traverse in 1939, and became an elaborate planter.

THE CHURCHYARD & ABBEY GARDENS

THE RUINS C1955 B258016

This photograph shows the dovecote at the end of the Abbot's garden, the wall of which is undergoing repairs at the time of the picture. The unexcavated ruins of the Abbot's Palace can be seen to the right.

THE ABBEY GARDENS, THE ROSE GARDEN C1955 B258041

This shows the garden within a few years of planting. The chancel of the cathedral was designed by Sir George Gilbert Scott, and was built between 1865 and 1869.

THE CHURCHYARD & ABBEY GARDENS

ABOVE: KING EDWARD'S GRAMMAR SCHOOL 1898 41244

The school was designed by Sir Arthur Bloomfield in 1883; it contained the Headmaster's residence, boarding accommodation and classrooms, including the 'Big School', later the library, on the ground floor. To the right are the fives courts and gymnasium of 1892, later the dayboys' dining hall. The left side of the building including the central gable was converted into flats, and the remainder was demolished in the 1980s.

RIGHT: THE ABBEY GARDENS
1898 41231

This view is taken from the Vinefields side of the river, on the footpath leading from the Grammar School into the Abbey Gardens. The bridge was built and the footpath laid down in 1883. This part of the gardens seems to have been let for grazing; the unexcavated Abbey church lies behind the horse.

THE CHURCHYARD & ABBEY GARDENS

ABOVE: THE RIVER LARK 1929
81942

Taken from the Grammar School bridge, this tranquil view shows the gardens in their role as a public park, with visitors watching the swans and sitting in the sun.

LEFT: THE ABBOT'S BRIDGE C1955
B258037

The 12th-century bridge, with later additions, is a continuation of the precinct wall linking Eastgate Street with the Vinefields. The arches once had portcullises into the water, and there is a walkway on the inside of the wall.

CHURCHES, HOUSES & NEW DEVELOPMENTS

n the 18th century there were two Anglican parish churches, a Catholic chapel and four Nonconformist places of worship. In the first half of the 19th century, as the population increased by 45%, the places of worship increased to four Anglican churches, a Catholic chapel of 1838 in Westgate Street, and nine Nonconformist chapels. St John's Church, and the chapels for the Primitive Methodists, Baptists and Plymouth Brethren were all built to the north; St Peter's Church and the Strict Baptist Chapel were built to the west of the medieval town, in the expanding areas of new housing.

The places of Nonconformist worship were the Unitarian Chapel of 1711 in Churchgate Street, and two Congregational chapels, one of 1716 in Whiting Street, the other of 1828 in Northgate Street, which was rebuilt in 1866 and became the Primitive Methodist Chapel from 1902 to 1934. The Quaker Meeting House of 1752 is in St John's Street; a Wesleyan Methodist Chapel of 1811 was in St Mary's Square, on the site of a house where John Wesley preached 17 times between 1755 and 1790. This was replaced in 1873 by Trinity Church in Brentgovel Street. A Primitive Methodist Chapel of 1830 in Garland Street was sold to the Plymouth Brethren in 1853, after a new one had been built in 1851; the Baptist Chapel opened in Garland Street in 1834, replacing the earlier chapel of 1800 in Lower Baxter Street, where the burial ground survives; and a Strict Baptist Chapel in Westgate Street opened in 1840.

St John's (41241, p76) was built in 1841 in the district where the railway station was to be opened in 1846-47. The design, by William Ranger, was in the 13th-century Early English style. It is built in white brick; its spire, 178ft high, is a landmark for miles around.

St Peter's (41243, p78) was built in 1856 near the hospital and workhouse. It was designed by John Hakewill, also in the Early English style and with a spire. The two churches had distinctly different theological styles - St John's was High and St Peter's was Low Church.

After the arrival of the railway, the population declined by 4% to 13,318 in 1861 and then stagnated at around 16,500 from 1881 until after World War II. In this period new churches were established near the railway. The Salvation Army opened their Citadel in St John's Street in 1893, and the Railway Mission opened in Fornham Road in 1895. In 1939 the Plymouth Brethren moved out to one of the suburbs at West Road, where they remain today in

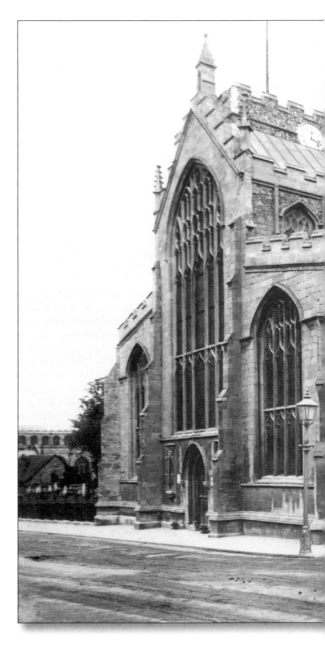

a modern church opened in 1992.

The first Local Authority houses were built at Grove Park in 1918-19, the Perry Barn Estate (later Priors) started in 1927, and the Priors Inn opened in 1933. In the post-war period the historic town has been virtually surrounded by housing, industrial and leisure developments. The first area of expansion was the Mildenhall Estate, begun in 1946-47, followed by the Howard and Westley Estates in

CHURCHES, HOUSES & NEW DEVELOPMENTS

ST MARY'S CHURCH 1898 41239

The church, except for the tower and chancel, was rebuilt by William Layer in c1424-45. The south porch was removed for road widening in 1831, and is now a folly at Nowton Park. How open and uncluttered the view is without the proliferation of modern traffic signs, those gates and tourist directions.

the 1960s and 1970s; these were partly funded by London overspill initiatives. These three estates were built on land to the north and west, which was taken in from the parishes of Fornham All Saints and Westley in 1934. Then in the late 1960s and 1970s came the Flemyng Road and Horringer Court developments to the west of the town. The Nowton, Mayfield Road and Home Farm Lane areas in the south-east were all built at the same time.

The dualling of the A45 (A14) in the early 1970s, which in 1972 gave Bury a by-pass through rather than round the town, created a direct route from the Midlands to Ipswich and Felixstowe. This gave the impetus for the eastern development of the Moreton Hall and associated estates, which began in the late 1970s and continues into the new millennium. Tim Brinton was the first business to be opened there in 1977, a year or so before the housing started.

CHURCHES, HOUSES & NEW DEVELOPMENTS

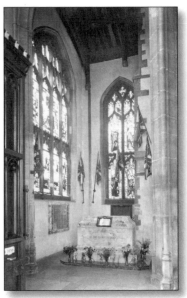

ABOVE: ST MARY'S CHURCH, THE INTERIOR 1922 71962

This photograph shows the magnificent hammer-beam roof of c1445, the Star of David St Edmund window of 1844 copied from the Abbey Gate, and the rood screen, which was erected as a Boer War Memorial in 1913. At the end of the south aisle is the cadaver tomb of John Baret (d1467) under a unique roof with reflective mirrors. Princess Mary Tudor, sister of Henry VIII, Queen of France and Duchess of Suffolk, after whom the ship 'Mary Rose' was named, died in 1533 and is buried within the sanctuary. St Mary's is the Civic Church, and hosts all state and commemorative services.

ABOVE RIGHT: ST MARY'S CHURCH, THE SUFFOLK WAR MEMORIAL 1929 81954

St Mary's was the Suffolk's regimental church; their war memorial was dedicated in 1920. To commemorate 300 years of the regiment in 1935, the north chapel was converted into the Suffolk Chapel, designed by Sir Ninian Comper.

RIGHT: ST JOHN'S CHURCH, THE INTERIOR 1898 41241

The Early English-style interior has arcade columns of cast iron and a continous roof in timber-ribbed vaulting. The elaborate stone and marble reredos is by J D Wyatt, 1875, and the window is by Forest and Bradley of Liverpool, 1886.

CHURCHES, HOUSES & NEW DEVELOPMENTS

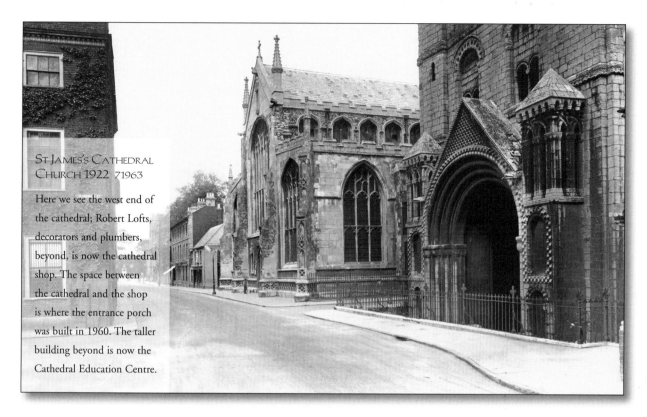

St James's Cathedral
Church 1922 71963

Here we see the west end of
the cathedral; Robert Lofts,
decorators and plumbers,
beyond, is now the cathedral
shop. The space between
the cathedral and the shop
is where the entrance porch
was built in 1960. The taller
building beyond is now the
Cathedral Education Centre.

The rapid rise in population (up 47% between 1951 and 2001) outstripped that of the first half of the 19th century. The increase from 20,056 in 1951 to 32,774 in 1991 and an estimated 35,000 in 2001 resulted in a wide range of leisure facilities being established. These included an athletics track, a sports and leisure centre, opened by Sir Alf Ramsey in 1975 and rebuilt in 1981, Rollerbury, opened in 1982, Nowton Park, and numerous sports, interests and amenity groups and societies.

With all the new housing developments went industrial and trading estates (the first was Western Way in 1955), schools, shops and places of worship. On the Mildenhall and Howard estates St George's Church opened in 1951, Northumberland Methodist Church and Lancaster Hall both opened in 1957, and the Pentecostal church in 1984. To serve the Priors and Horringer Court area, All Saints' was established in 1953 and the Horringer Court Fellowship in 1969. On the Nowton Estate, Southgate began in 1974 as an ecumenical church supported by the Bury Council of Churches. Christ Church, although an Anglican parish created in 1994, also works on an ecumenical basis in the Moreton Hall area.

A major change in the status of Bury was the creation, in 1914, of the new Diocese of St Edmundsbury and Ipswich. St James's (71963, above and 41235 p80) became the cathedral with a resident Provost, now a Dean, whilst the Bishop lived at Ipswich. The architect Stephen Dykes Bower drew up plans in 1956 for the extension of the church in a traditional gothic style, and the creation of a cathedral close. In the 1960s and 70s a new west porch, library, cloister, crossing and choir were built. These were followed in 1990 by the song school, refectory, treasury and lecture rooms.

In 1995 Stephen Dykes Bower left £2.7 million towards the cost of finishing the cathedral, including the central crossing tower. In 1998 the Millennium Commission agreed to contribute £5.15 million, and by mid 2000 the balance of £2.5 million had been raised locally. Work began on the 150ft central tower at the turn of the year 2000. The tower will change the skyline of Bury forever. It will probably be the last Gothic cathedral to be built, and will certainly be one of the great Christian commemorations of the Millennium.

CHURCHES, HOUSES & NEW DEVELOPMENTS

ABOVE: ST PETER'S CHURCH 1895 41243

Built in 1856, the church has the crossed keys of St Peter below the east window. Behind the church are the hospital of 1826 and the birthplace of the Victorian novelist Ouida (1839-1907). A monument to her stands at the junction of Westgate Street and Vinery Road. In the distance is the Thingoe Union workhouse of 1836, which also served Bury after 1884. The workhouse closed in 1929 and eventually became St Mary's geriatric hospital until 1977.

RIGHT: THE HOSPITAL AND ST PETER'S CHURCH C1965 B258083

This road is still open to Westgate Street and has two-way traffic. The balconies on the hospital were added in 1908.

Churches, Houses & New Developments

CHURCHES, HOUSES & NEW DEVELOPMENTS

ABOVE: ST JAMES'S CATHEDRAL CHURCH AND THE NORMAN TOWER 1898   41235

The width of the pathway in this photograph compared with the width today shows how much further east the choir was rebuilt in the 1960s

ABOVE RIGHT: ST JAMES'S CATHEDRAL CHURCH AND THE NORMAN TOWER c1955   B258010

This photograph shows the churchyard just before the removal of the monuments in 1958, although the rails have already been removed.

RIGHT CENTRE: THE CATHEDRAL c1965   B258074

The monuments have been removed, and the area has been laid to lawn. On the right, we see evidence of the building work which was under way from 1964 to 1970. The chapel on the side of the chancel now forms part of the transept of the crossing.

CHURCHES, HOUSES & NEW DEVELOPMENTS

This shows the early 16th-century nave and aisle designed by John Wastell, the architect of King's College, Cambridge. Sir George Scott designed the hammer-beam roof and the chancel (1865-69). The chancel was demolished in the 1960s, when the new choir and crossing were begun. The building of the central crossing tower is now under way, and should be completed in 2003.

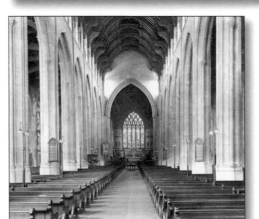

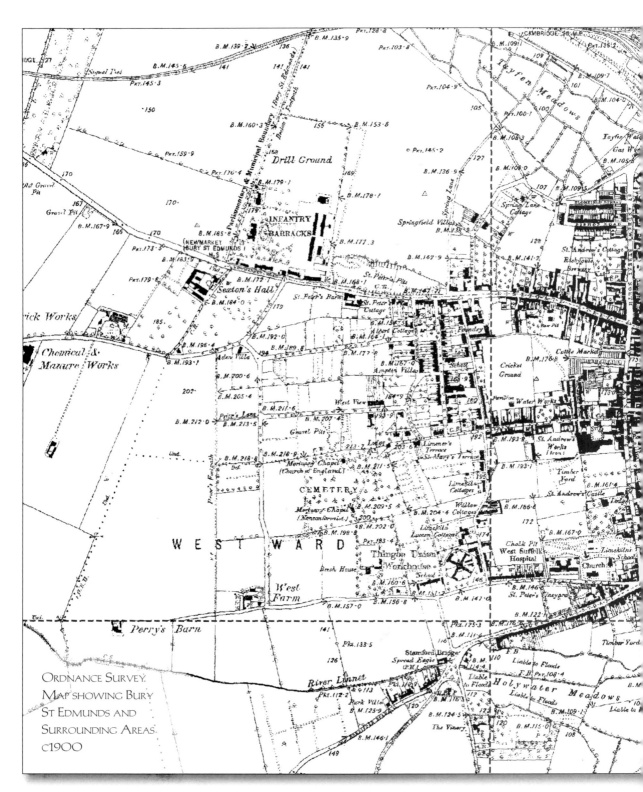

ORDNANCE SURVEY
MAP SHOWING BURY
ST EDMUNDS AND
SURROUNDING AREAS.
c1900

INDEX

Frith Book Co Titles

www.francisfrith.co.uk

The Frith Book Company publishes over 100 new titles each year. A selection of those currently available is listed below. For latest catalogue please contact Frith Book Co.
Town Books 96 pages, approximately 100 photos. **County and Themed Books** 128 pages, approximately 150 photos (unless specified). All titles hardback with laminated case and jacket, except those indicated pb (paperback)

Amersham, Chesham & Rickmansworth (pb)	1-85937-340-2	£9.99	Devon (pb)	1-85937-297-x	£9.99
Andover (pb)	1-85937-292-9	£9.99	Devon Churches (pb)	1-85937-250-3	£9.99
Aylesbury (pb)	1-85937-227-9	£9.99	Dorchester (pb)	1-85937-307-0	£9.99
Barnstaple (pb)	1-85937-300-3	£9.99	Dorset (pb)	1-85937-269-4	£9.99
Basildon Living Memories (pb)	1-85937-515-4	£9.99	Dorset Coast (pb)	1-85937-299-6	£9.99
Bath (pb)	1-85937-419-0	£9.99	Dorset Living Memories (pb)	1-85937-584-7	£9.99
Bedford (pb)	1-85937-205-8	£9.99	Down the Severn (pb)	1-85937-560-x	£9.99
Bedfordshire Living Memories	1-85937-513-8	£14.99	Down The Thames (pb)	1-85937-278-3	£9.99
Belfast (pb)	1-85937-303-8	£9.99	Down the Trent	1-85937-311-9	£14.99
Berkshire (pb)	1-85937-191-4	£9.99	East Anglia (pb)	1-85937-265-1	£9.99
Berkshire Churches	1-85937-170-1	£17.99	East Grinstead (pb)	1-85937-138-8	£9.99
Berkshire Living Memories	1-85937-332-1	£14.99	East London	1-85937-080-2	£14.99
Black Country	1-85937-497-2	£12.99	East Sussex (pb)	1-85937-606-1	£9.99
Blackpool (pb)	1-85937-393-3	£9.99	Eastbourne (pb)	1-85937-399-2	£9.99
Bognor Regis (pb)	1-85937-431-x	£9.99	Edinburgh (pb)	1-85937-193-0	£8.99
Bournemouth (pb)	1-85937-545-6	£9.99	England In The 1880s	1-85937-331-3	£17.99
Bradford (pb)	1-85937-204-x	£9.99	Essex - Second Selection	1-85937-456-5	£14.99
Bridgend (pb)	1-85937-386-0	£7.99	Essex (pb)	1-85937-270-8	£9.99
Bridgwater (pb)	1-85937-305-4	£9.99	Essex Coast	1-85937-342-9	£14.99
Bridport (pb)	1-85937-327-5	£9.99	Essex Living Memories	1-85937-490-5	£14.99
Brighton (pb)	1-85937-192-2	£8.99	Exeter	1-85937-539-1	£9.99
Bristol (pb)	1-85937-264-3	£9.99	Exmoor (pb)	1-85937-608-8	£9.99
British Life A Century Ago (pb)	1-85937-213-9	£9.99	Falmouth (pb)	1-85937-594-4	£9.99
Buckinghamshire (pb)	1-85937-200-7	£9.99	Folkestone (pb)	1-85937-124-8	£9.99
Camberley (pb)	1-85937-222-8	£9.99	Frome (pb)	1-85937-317-8	£9.99
Cambridge (pb)	1-85937-422-0	£9.99	Glamorgan	1-85937-488-3	£14.99
Cambridgeshire (pb)	1-85937-420-4	£9.99	Glasgow (pb)	1-85937-190-6	£9.99
Cambridgeshire Villages	1-85937-523-5	£14.99	Glastonbury (pb)	1-85937-338-0	£7.99
Canals And Waterways (pb)	1-85937-291-0	£9.99	Gloucester (pb)	1-85937-232-5	£9.99
Canterbury Cathedral (pb)	1-85937-179-5	£9.99	Gloucestershire (pb)	1-85937-561-8	£9.99
Cardiff (pb)	1-85937-093-4	£9.99	Great Yarmouth (pb)	1-85937-426-3	£9.99
Carmarthenshire (pb)	1-85937-604-5	£9.99	Greater Manchester (pb)	1-85937-266-x	£9.99
Chelmsford (pb)	1-85937-310-0	£9.99	Guildford (pb)	1-85937-410-7	£9.99
Cheltenham (pb)	1-85937-095-0	£9.99	Hampshire (pb)	1-85937-279-1	£9.99
Cheshire (pb)	1-85937-271-6	£9.99	Harrogate (pb)	1-85937-423-9	£9.99
Chester (pb)	1-85937-382 8	£9.99	Hastings and Bexhill (pb)	1-85937-131-0	£9.99
Chesterfield (pb)	1-85937-378-x	£9.99	Heart of Lancashire (pb)	1-85937-197-3	£9.99
Chichester (pb)	1-85937-228-7	£9.99	Helston (pb)	1-85937-214-7	£9.99
Churches of East Cornwall (pb)	1-85937-249-x	£9.99	Hereford (pb)	1-85937-175-2	£9.99
Churches of Hampshire (pb)	1-85937-207-4	£9.99	Herefordshire (pb)	1-85937-567-7	£9.99
Cinque Ports & Two Ancient Towns	1-85937-492-1	£14.99	Herefordshire Living Memories	1-85937-514-6	£14.99
Colchester (pb)	1-85937-188-4	£8.99	Hertfordshire (pb)	1-85937-247-3	£9.99
Cornwall (pb)	1-85937-229-5	£9.99	Horsham (pb)	1-85937-432-8	£9.99
Cornwall Living Memories	1-85937-248-1	£14.99	Humberside (pb)	1-85937-605-3	£9.99
Cotswolds (pb)	1-85937-230-9	£9.99	Hythe, Romney Marsh, Ashford (pb)	1-85937-256-2	£9.99
Cotswolds Living Memories	1-85937-255-4	£14.99	Ipswich (pb)	1-85937-424-7	£9.99
County Durham (pb)	1-85937-398-4	£9.99	Isle of Man (pb)	1-85937-268-6	£9.99
Croydon Living Memories (pb)	1-85937-162-0	£9.99	Isle of Wight (pb)	1-85937-429-8	£9.99
Cumbria (pb)	1-85937-621-5	£9.99	Isle of Wight Living Memories	1-85937-304-6	£14.99
Derby (pb)	1-85937-367-4	£9.99	Kent (pb)	1-85937-189-2	£9.99
Derbyshire (pb)	1-85937-196-5	£9.99	Kent Living Memories(pb)	1-85937-401-8	£9.99
Derbyshire Living Memories	1-85937-330-5	£14.99	Kings Lynn (pb)	1-85937-334-8	£9.99

Available from your local bookshop or from the publisher

Frith Book Co Titles (continued)

Title	ISBN	Price	Title	ISBN	Price
Lake District (pb)	1-85937-275-9	£9.99	Sherborne (pb)	1-85937-301-1	£9.99
Lancashire Living Memories	1-85937-335-6	£14.99	Shrewsbury (pb)	1-85937-325-9	£9.99
Lancaster, Morecambe, Heysham (pb)	1-85937-233-3	£9.99	Shropshire (pb)	1-85937-326-7	£9.99
Leeds (pb)	1-85937-202-3	£9.99	Shropshire Living Memories	1-85937-643-6	£14.99
Leicester (pb)	1-85937-381-x	£9.99	Somerset	1-85937-153-1	£14.99
Leicestershire & Rutland Living Memories	1-85937-500-6	£12.99	South Devon Coast	1-85937-107-8	£14.99
Leicestershire (pb)	1-85937-185-x	£9.99	South Devon Living Memories (pb)	1-85937-609-6	£9.99
Lighthouses	1-85937-257-0	£9.99	South East London (pb)	1-85937-263-5	£9.99
Lincoln (pb)	1-85937-380-1	£9.99	South Somerset	1-85937-318-6	£14.99
Lincolnshire (pb)	1-85937-433-6	£9.99	South Wales	1-85937-519-7	£14.99
Liverpool and Merseyside (pb)	1-85937-234-1	£9.99	Southampton	1-85937-427-1	£9.99
London (pb)	1-85937-183-3	£9.99	Southend (pb)	1-85937-313-5	£9.99
London Living Memories	1-85937-454-9	£14.99	Southport (pb)	1-85937-425-5	£9.99
Ludlow (pb)	1-85937-176-0	£9.99	St Albans (pb)	1-85937-341-0	£9.99
Luton (pb)	1-85937-235-x	£9.99	St Ives (pb)	1-85937-415-8	£9.99
Maidenhead (pb)	1-85937-339-9	£9.99	Stafford Living Memories (pb)	1-85937-503-0	£9.99
Maidstone (pb)	1-85937-391-7	£9.99	Staffordshire (pb)	1-85937-308-9	£9.99
Manchester (pb)	1-85937-198-1	£9.99	Stourbridge (pb)	1-85937-530-8	£9.99
Marlborough (pb)	1-85937-336-4	£9.99	Stratford upon Avon (pb)	1-85937-388-7	£9.99
Middlesex	1-85937-158-2	£14.99	Suffolk (pb)	1-85937-221-x	£9.99
Monmouthshire	1-85937-532-4	£14.99	Suffolk Coast (pb)	1-85937-610-x	£9.99
New Forest (pb)	1-85937-390-9	£9.99	Surrey (pb)	1-85937-240-6	£9.99
Newark (pb)	1-85937-366-6	£9.99	Surrey Living Memories	1-85937-328-3	£14.99
Newport, Wales (pb)	1-85937-258-9	£9.99	Sussex (pb)	1-85937-184-1	£9.99
Newquay (pb)	1-85937-421-2	£9.99	Sutton (pb)	1-85937-337-2	£9.99
Norfolk (pb)	1-85937-195-7	£9.99	Swansea (pb)	1-85937-167-1	£9.99
Norfolk Broads	1-85937-486-7	£14.99	Taunton (pb)	1-85937-314-3	£9.99
Norfolk Living Memories (pb)	1-85937-402-6	£9.99	Tees Valley & Cleveland (pb)	1-85937-623-1	£9.99
North Buckinghamshire	1-85937-626-6	£14.99	Teignmouth (pb)	1-85937-370-4	£7.99
North Devon Living Memories	1-85937-261-9	£14.99	Thanet (pb)	1-85937-116-7	£9.99
North Hertfordshire	1-85937-547-2	£14.99	Tiverton (pb)	1-85937-178-7	£9.99
North London (pb)	1-85937-403-4	£9.99	Torbay (pb)	1-85937-597-9	£9.99
North Somerset	1-85937-302-x	£14.99	Truro (pb)	1-85937-598-7	£9.99
North Wales (pb)	1-85937-298-8	£9.99	Victorian & Edwardian Dorset	1-85937-254-6	£14.99
North Yorkshire (pb)	1-85937-236-8	£9.99	Victorian & Edwardian Kent (pb)	1-85937-624-X	£9.99
Northamptonshire Living Memories	1-85937-529-4	£14.99	Victorian & Edwardian Maritime Album (pb)	1-85937-622-3	£9.99
Northamptonshire	1-85937-150-7	£14.99	Victorian and Edwardian Sussex (pb)	1-85937-625-8	£9.99
Northumberland Tyne & Wear (pb)	1-85937-281-3	£9.99	Villages of Devon (pb)	1-85937-293-7	£9.99
Northumberland	1-85937-522-7	£14.99	Villages of Kent (pb)	1-85937-294-5	£9.99
Norwich (pb)	1-85937-194-9	£8.99	Villages of Sussex (pb)	1-85937-295-3	£9.99
Nottingham (pb)	1-85937-324-0	£9.99	Warrington (pb)	1-85937-507-3	£9.99
Nottinghamshire (pb)	1-85937-187-6	£9.99	Warwick (pb)	1-85937-518-9	£9.99
Oxford (pb)	1-85937-411-5	£9.99	Warwickshire (pb)	1-85937-203-1	£9.99
Oxfordshire (pb)	1-85937-430-1	£9.99	Welsh Castles (pb)	1-85937-322-4	£9.99
Oxfordshire Living Memories	1-85937-525-1	£14.99	West Midlands (pb)	1-85937-289-9	£9.99
Paignton (pb)	1-85937-374-7	£7.99	West Sussex (pb)	1-85937-607-x	£9.99
Peak District (pb)	1-85937-280-5	£9.99	West Yorkshire (pb)	1-85937-201-5	£9.99
Pembrokeshire	1-85937-262-7	£14.99	Weston Super Mare (pb)	1-85937-306-2	£9.99
Penzance (pb)	1-85937-595-2	£9.99	Weymouth (pb)	1-85937-209-0	£9.99
Peterborough (pb)	1-85937-219-8	£9.99	Wiltshire (pb)	1-85937-277-5	£9.99
Picturesque Harbours	1-85937-208-2	£14.99	Wiltshire Churches (pb)	1-85937-171-x	£9.99
Piers	1-85937-237-6	£17.99	Wiltshire Living Memories (pb)	1-85937-396-8	£9.99
Plymouth (pb)	1-85937-389-5	£9.99	Winchester (pb)	1-85937-428-x	£9.99
Poole & Sandbanks (pb)	1-85937-251-1	£9.99	Windsor (pb)	1-85937-333-x	£9.99
Preston (pb)	1-85937-212-0	£9.99	Wokingham & Bracknell (pb)	1-85937-329-1	£9.99
Reading (pb)	1-85937-238-4	£9.99	Woodbridge (pb)	1-85937-498-0	£9.99
Redhill to Reigate (pb)	1-85937-596-0	£9.99	Worcester (pb)	1-85937-165-5	£9.99
Ringwood (pb)	1-85937-384-4	£7.99	Worcestershire Living Memories	1-85937-489-1	£14.99
Romford (pb)	1-85937-319-4	£9.99	Worcestershire	1-85937-152-3	£14.99
Royal Tunbridge Wells (pb)	1-85937-504-9	£9.99	York (pb)	1-85937-199-x	£9.99
Salisbury (pb)	1-85937-239-2	£9.99	Yorkshire (pb)	1-85937-186-8	£9.99
Scarborough (pb)	1-85937-379-8	£9.99	Yorkshire Coastal Memories	1-85937-506-5	£14.99
Sevenoaks and Tonbridge (pb)	1-85937-392-5	£9.99	Yorkshire Dales	1-85937-502-2	£14.99
Sheffield & South Yorks (pb)	1-85937-267-8	£9.99	Yorkshire Living Memories (pb)	1-85937-397-6	£9.99

See Frith books on the internet at www.francisfrith.co.uk

FRITH PRODUCTS & SERVICES

Francis Frith would doubtless be pleased to know that the pioneering publishing venture he started in 1860 still continues today. Over a hundred and forty years later, The Francis Frith Collection continues in the same innovative tradition and is now one of the foremost publishers of vintage photographs in the world. Some of the current activities include:

Interior Decoration

Today Frith's photographs can be seen framed and as giant wall murals in thousands of pubs, restaurants, hotels, banks, retail stores and other public buildings throughout the country. In every case they enhance the unique local atmosphere of the places they depict and provide reminders of gentler days in an increasingly busy and frenetic world.

Product Promotions

Frith products are used by many major companies to promote the sales of their own products or to reinforce their own history and heritage. Frith promotions have been used by Hovis bread, Courage beers, Scots Porage Oats, Colman's mustard, Cadbury's foods, Mellow Birds coffee, Dunhill pipe tobacco, Guinness, and Bulmer's Cider.

Genealogy and Family History

As the interest in family history and roots grows world-wide, more and more people are turning to Frith's photographs of Great Britain for images of the towns, villages and streets where their ancestors lived; and, of course, photographs of the churches and chapels where their ancestors were christened, married and buried are an essential part of every genealogy tree and family album.

Frith Products

All Frith photographs are available Framed or just as Mounted Prints and Posters (size 23 x 16 inches). These may be ordered from the address below. From time to time other products - Address Books, Calendars, Table Mats, etc - are available.

The Internet

Already fifty thousand Frith photographs can be viewed and purchased on the internet through the Frith websites and a myriad of partner sites.

For more detailed information on Frith companies and products, look at these sites:

www.francisfrith.co.uk
www.francisfrith.com
(for North American visitors)

See the complete list of Frith Books at:

www.francisfrith.co.uk

This web site is regularly updated with the latest list of publications from the Frith Book Company. If you wish to buy books relating to another part of the country that your local bookshop does not stock, you may purchase on-line.

For further information, trade, or author enquiries please contact us at the address below:
The Francis Frith Collection, Frith's Barn, Teffont, Salisbury, Wiltshire, England SP3 5QP.
Tel: +44 (0)1722 716 376   Fax: +44 (0)1722 716 881   Email: sales@francisfrith.co.uk

See Frith books on the internet at www.francisfrith.co.uk

FREE PRINT OF YOUR CHOICE

Mounted Print
Overall size 14 x 11 inches (355 x 280mm)

Choose any Frith photograph in this book.
Simply complete the Voucher opposite and return it with your remittance for £2.25 (to cover postage and handling) and we will print the photograph of your choice in SEPIA (size 11 x 8 inches) and supply it in a cream mount with a burgundy rule line (overall size 14 x 11 inches).
Please note: photographs with a reference number starting with a "Z" are not Frith photographs and cannot be supplied under this offer.
Offer valid for delivery to one UK address only.

PLUS: Order additional Mounted Prints at HALF PRICE - £7.49 each (normally £14.99)
If you would like to order more Frith prints from this book, possibly as gifts for friends and family, you can buy them at half price (with no additional postage and handling costs).

PLUS: Have your Mounted Prints framed
For an extra £14.95 per print you can have your mounted print(s) framed in an elegant polished wood and gilt moulding, overall size 16 x 13 inches (no additional postage and handling required).

IMPORTANT!

These special prices are only available if you use this form to order . You must use the ORIGINAL VOUCHER on this page (no copies permitted). We can only despatch to one UK address. This offer cannot be combined with any other offer.

Send completed Voucher form to:
The Francis Frith Collection, Frith's Barn, Teffont, Salisbury, Wiltshire SP3 5QP

CHOOSE A PHOTOGRAPH FROM THIS BOOK

Voucher for *FREE* and Reduced Price Frith Prints

Please do not photocopy this voucher. Only the original is valid, so please fill it in, cut it out and return it to us with your order.

Picture ref no	Page no	Qty	Mounted @ £7.49	Framed + £14.95	Total Cost £
		1	Free of charge*	£	£
			£7.49	£	£
			£7.49	£	£
			£7.49	£	£
			£7.49	£	£
			£7.49	£	£

Please allow 28 days for delivery. Offer available to one UK address only

* Post & handling	£2.25
Total Order Cost	£

Title of this book . . . .
I enclose a cheque/postal order for £ . . . .
made payable to 'The Francis Frith Collection'

OR please debit my Mastercard / Visa / Maestro / Amex card, details below

Card Number

Issue No (Maestro only)   Valid from (Maestro)

Expires   Signature

Name Mr/Mrs/Ms . . . .
Address . . . .
. . . .
. . . .
. . . . Postcode . . . .
Daytime Tel No . . . .
Email . . . .

1-84589-081-7   Valid to 31/12/07

Free Print – see overleaf

Would you like to find out more about Francis Frith?

We have recently recruited some entertaining speakers who are happy to visit local groups, clubs and societies to give an illustrated talk documenting Frith's travels and photographs. If you are a member of such a group and are interested in hosting a presentation, we would love to hear from you.

Our speakers bring with them a small selection of our local town and county books, together with sample prints. They are happy to take orders. A small proportion of the order value is donated to the group who have hosted the presentation. The talks are therefore an excellent way of fundraising for small groups and societies.

Can you help us with information about any of the Frith photographs in this book?

We are gradually compiling an historical record for each of the photographs in the Frith archive. It is always fascinating to find out the names of the people shown in the pictures, as well as insights into the shops, buildings and other features depicted.

If you recognize anyone in the photographs in this book, or if you have information not already included in the author's caption, do let us know. We would love to hear from you, and will try to publish it in future books or articles.

Our production team

Frith books are produced by a small dedicated team at offices in the converted Grade II listed 18th-century barn at Teffont near Salisbury, illustrated above. Most have worked with the Frith Collection for many years. All have in common one quality: they have a passion for the Frith Collection. The team is constantly expanding, but currently includes:

Paul Baron, Phillip Brennan, Jason Buck, John Buck, Ruth Butler, Heather Crisp, David Davies, Louis du Mont, Isobel Hall, Lucy Hart, Julian Hight, Peter Horne, James Kinnear, Karen Kinnear, Tina Leary, Stuart Login, David Marsh, Lesley-Ann Millard, Sue Molloy, Glenda Morgan, Wayne Morgan, Sarah Roberts, Kate Rotondetto, Dean Scource, Eliza Sackett, Terence Sackett, Sandra Sampson, Adrian Sanders, Sandra Sanger, Jan Scrivens, Julia Skinner, Miles Smith, Lewis Taylor, Shelley Tolcher, Lorraine Tuck, Amanita Wainwright and Ricky Williams.